KS2 national tests

Science

preparation and practice
for use at home

Lillian Wright
Primary Science Advisor

ISBN 0 563 47419 X

Published by BBC Educational Publishing

First Published in 1999
Reprinted in 2000

© Lillian Wright/BBC Worldwide (Educational Publishing), 1999

All rights reserved. No part of this publication may be reproduces, stored in any form or by means mechanical, electronic recording or otherwise without prior permission of the publisher.

Acknowledgement to Steve Pollock for extract from *Find Out About Animals* (BBC Educational Publishing)

Reproduced and printed in Great Britain by sterling

Page Design by Malena Wilson-Max at Tribal Design

Illustrations by Tribal Design

Contents

Introduction	4
📺 🌐 **Overview of the test**	6-9
Using clues on the page	6
Spot the mistakes	8
📺 🌐 **The skills you need**	10-11
Answering questions	10
BIOLOGY	
📺 **Living things in their environment**	12-15
🌐 Researching habitats	12
🌐 Microbes and decay	14
Humans and other animals	16-19
🌐 What do you know about teeth?	16
🌐 Human growth	17
🌐 Taking a pulse	18
Drugs and health	19
📺 **Green plants**	20-22
🌐 Growing plants from seed	20
Variety in plants	21
CHEMISTRY	
📺 **Grouping and classifying materials**	23-26
🌐 Classifying materials	23
Investigating magnetism and electricity	24
📺 Solids, liquids and gases	25
🌐 Evaporation in everyday life	26
Changing materials	27-28
🌐 Making a solution	27
🌐 Reversible and irreversible changes	28
Separating materials	29
🌐 Separating a mixture	29
PHYSICS	
Electricity	30-31
🌐 Electricity drawings and symbols	30
🌐 Looking at switches	31
Forces	32-33
🌐 Looking at friction	32
🌐 Know your forces	33
Forces and measurement	34-35
🌐 Investigating forces	34
🌐 Pushing and pulling	35
📺 🌐 **Light**	36-37
Investigating light	36
A closer look at light	37
📺 **Sound**	38-39
🌐 Making noise	38
Good vibrations	39
📺 **The Earth and beyond**	40-41
🌐 The Earth in space	40
Sun, Earth and Moon	41
Answers to activities and guidance	42

📺 Means a link to the TV
🌐 Means a link to the website

Introduction for parents

What is Key Stage 2 ReviseWise?

In May, Year 6 pupils take their Key Stage 2 (KS2) National Tests in Science, Maths and English. The Tests show teachers what level children are working at to help in their move to secondary school. This book is part of the BBC's Key Stage 2 ReviseWise service, created to help children get ready to do their best in all their KS2 National Tests.

For KS2 Science there are two Tests, A and B, which are 35 minutes long each. Both Tests contain work from the whole science curriculum and are the same level of difficulty. There is a harder extension paper, but your child's teacher will have told you if your child is entered for this. The KS2 ReviseWise Science resources are:

- this book
- television programme that you can video
- a ready-made video to buy
- a CD-ROM
- a website.

The ReviseWise Science resources have been developed and written by specialists to help children working through level 3 to levels 4 and 5. ReviseWise covers the key areas of Science which will be tested.

If your child uses all the elements of ReviseWise, there's such a variety of things to do that revising need never be boring. There are even ReviseWise resources for schools, so there's a link between home and school learning.

How to get the most out of Key Stage 2 ReviseWise

- Help your child to work through this book to practise Test-style questions. There are lots of 'Wise-up' tips to help with the answers and give advice.
- Encourage your child to watch (and re-watch) the video of eight 15-minute sections on Science. They bring the subject to life and explain what the Tests are all about.
- Is your child always glued to the computer? The CD-ROM takes children through questions step-by-step, with as much – or as little – help as they need along the way.
- If you're on the Internet, your child can visit the website for more learning fun. There's also a special section to help parents get to grips with the Tests and revision.

Useful links

There are symbols next to topic headings in this book to show your child where there are links to other parts of the ReviseWise service.

📺 means a link to the television programme

🌐 means a link to the website

Using this book

Each activity page in this book offers Test-style questions, puzzles or activities which will help children confirm what they know and practise their skills in Science ready for the KS2 Tests. The main points they need to know are highlighted at the top of each page, followed by the sorts of question-and-answer activities they will meet in the Test. Some things may seem different from when you learned them. Ask your child's teacher if you're not sure.

Children can work steadily through the book, or head straight for the activities they know they need more practice in. At the end of each activity, children can record their progress. They can circle, tick or colour one of these pictures that appear at the side of the page:

 I know this   Come back to this   Ask my teacher

Then it's easy to skim back through the book and see which activities they need to have another go at, or to ask their teacher for a little more help with.

If children do the activities in this book in pencil, they can do them again later, either for repeat practice, or if they get any answers wrong. They can also keep track of how much work they have done by ticking or colouring the shapes on the big ReviseWise Owl at the back of this book.

Answers

The Answers section at the back of this book gives the correct answers to the questions. They also give you an idea of the level the question is aimed at, so that you can get some indication of the level your child is reaching.

Please remember, though, that the level you feel that your child achieves by answering the questions in this book can only be a general indication of the actual level he or she may achieve in the Tests.

KS2 ReviseWise Science 5

Using clues on the page

Wise up!

To do your best in the test, remember this:
- make sure you take time to read the questions carefully.

On the actual question paper:
- each question is written in a shaded area
- a pencil symbol, like this ✎, shows you where to write your answers
- the size of the space you are given to write your answers in shows you how long your answer should be
- you will be asked to interpret information from pictures, tables and graphs.

Activity

Try answering the questions on this page and page 7. Look for the clues that tell you **how much to write** and **where to write your answer**.

1 Look at the drawings of four seeds.

  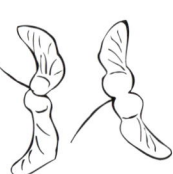 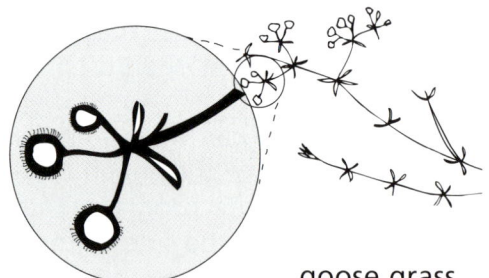

sweet chestnut   clematis   field maple   goose grass

> Which **TWO** seeds are dispersed (moved from the parent plant) by the wind?

✎ .... and ....

2 Anna and Sam dropped different-sized pieces of paper down a stairwell. They watched to see which piece of paper fell the most slowly.

> Explain, in terms of forces, why the smallest piece of paper took the shortest time to fall.

✎ ....
....
....
....

6 KS2 ReviseWise Science

This activity continues on the next page

3 Look at the graph on the right.
How long did it take for the seedlings to grow 4cm tall?

....

Graph to show growth of radish seedlings

4 Smoking cigarettes can be bad for your health.
Name **TWO** organs of your body that may be damaged by cigarette smoking.

.... and

....

Some children tested different objects with a magnet. They made a table of their results. Look at the table and then answer question 5.

Name of object	Attracted to the magnet?
paperclip	yes
plastic ruler	no
metal scissors	yes
pencil	no
aluminium drink can	no
gold ring	no

The questions in the rest of this book don't appear in shaded areas nor will you see the pencil symbol. Watch out for them in the Test though.

5 Explain why some of the objects are not attracted to the magnet.

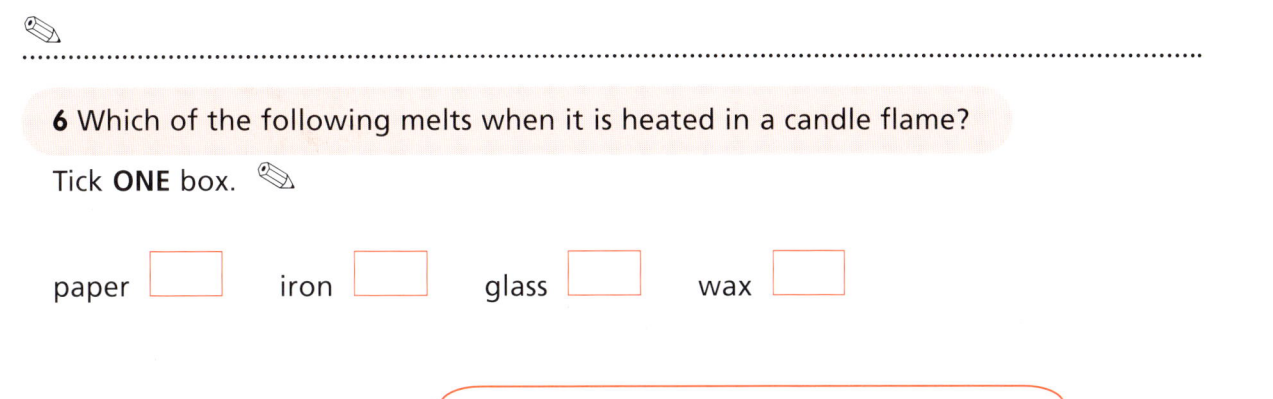

....

6 Which of the following melts when it is heated in a candle flame?
Tick **ONE** box.

paper ☐   iron ☐   glass ☐   wax ☐

Have you answered all the questions?

Spot the mistakes

Wise up!

Avoid making silly mistakes in the test by:
- making sure you can see where to write answers, how much to write and how many boxes to tick
- knowing what particular words mean when they are used in science questions
- looking out for how many marks you will gain for answering the question correctly.

Activity

Look at questions 1–4 on this page and page 9. Someone has answered questions 1–4 but there is something wrong with the answers. On the dotted lines by the questions, write what is wrong and what the answer should be.

1 What happens when ice is heated?
Tick **TWO** boxes.

It melts	✓
It condenses	✓
It turns to slush	
It becomes a liquid	✓
It becomes a solid	

.... 1

.... 1

....

2 Write **ONE** word to describe the change from liquid to gas.

   It's when a liquid gets enough energy to become water vapour.

....

.... 1

3 Write the name of **ONE** producer from the food chains below.

   grass → rabbit → fox   cabbage → caterpillar → bird

   Cabbage and caterpillar.

....

.... 1

This activity continues on the next page

8 KS2 ReviseWise Science

4 Write **Yes** or **No** in the table below.

Object	Is it flexible?
aluminium foil	✓
pencil	No
plastic bag	It might be
glass	✗
silk	Yes

Remember, you are looking for two things: what is wrong and what the answer should be.

[1]

....

[1]

....

5 Look back at questions 1, 2, 3 and 4.

How many marks do you gain if you answer correctly:

a) Question 1 .... c) Question 3 ....

b) Question 2 .... d) Question 4 ....

6 How did you know this?

....

7 Tick the correct meaning below.

Explain means: write a description ☐

give a reason why something happened ☐

sort into groups ☐

compare one thing with another ☐

There are no mark boxes in this book, but you can check your answers in the back.

8 What do these words mean?

a) describe ....

b) compare ....

c) complete ....

Have you answered all the questions?

Answering questions

Wise up!

To answer questions well, remember that:
- information can come from secondary sources, such as books, CD-ROMs, the Internet, videos and television
- you can review the work of others and describe its value and faults
- information can come from your own experiences and observations
- to carry out a fair test, one factor must be changed and the effects observed, while keeping other factors the same
- you can record results in many different ways
- recording results allows you to make comparisons and helps you explain what you find out
- you should repeat tests to check your observations and measurements.

Activity

It's a good idea to watch videos and television programmes about science and use CD-ROMs, the Internet and reference books to learn more about science and the world around you.

Read this extract from a book about animals.

What do animals eat?

All animals must eat if they are to live. Some animals, like the snail, eat only plants. The snail feeds on green leaves. The blue tit eats both plants and animals. It feeds on seeds, nuts, fruit and insects. Other animals, like the tiger, eat meat. The tiger must catch its meat. It is called a predator. The animals it catches are called prey.

From *Find out about Animals* by Steve Pollock

Use the information in the text to answer the following questions.

1 Which life process is this extract about?

....

2 Which animal mentioned eats only plants?

....

3 Describe the diet of a blue tit.

....

4 What is the scientific term for an animal eaten by another animal?

....

This activity continues on the next page

Emily and Charlotte wanted to see if raising the height of a ramp would make a tennis ball travel further.

They held a tennis ball at the top of the ramp each time and then let go.

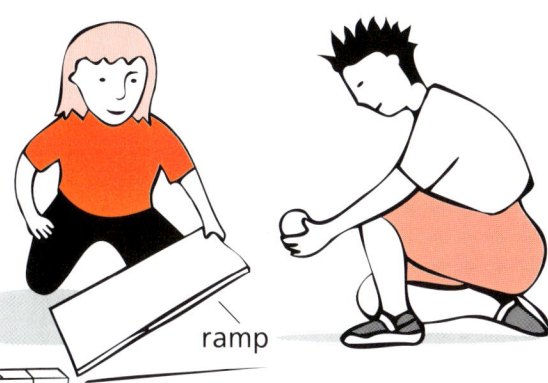

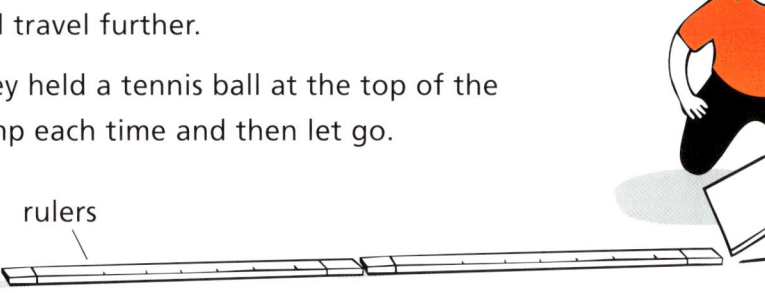

rulers

ramp

5 In their test, what factor did the children have to change each time?

....

6 What effect did they think it would have?

....

Here is a table of their results.

Height of ramp (cm)	Distance travelled by ball (m)			
	1st try	2nd try	3rd try	average distance (m)
10	1.5	1.3	1.35	1.38
20	2.1	1.6	2.05	1.91
30	3.0	2.7	2.7	2.80
40	4.1	3.8	3.85	3.92

Remember, they've tried to make their test as fair as possible.

7 Why did the children carry out the test 3 times at each height?

....

....

8 Charlotte wanted to use a cricket ball, for a change, half way through the test. Why wouldn't this be fair?

....

....

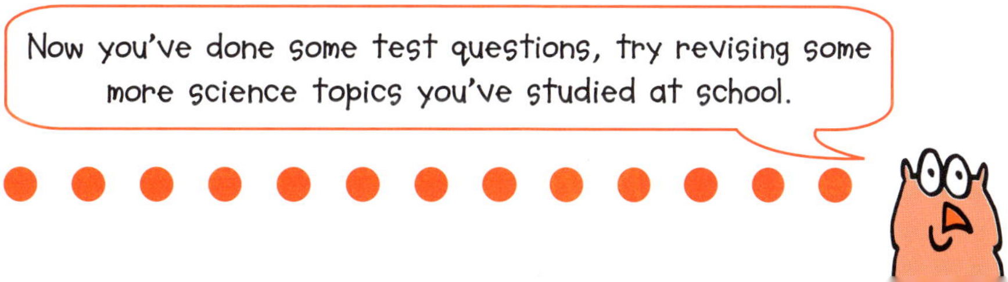

Now you've done some test questions, try revising some more science topics you've studied at school.

Researching habitats

Wise up!

When you are finding out about habitats:
- recognise that different animals live in different places
- record information in a table
- look for patterns in the data you collect
- remember that animals may feed on plants or other animals
- record feeding relationships as a **food chain**.

Activity

Go out into a garden or park on **two separate occasions**.

Look in **3 different places** for tiny animals. For instance, try:
- under a large stone or brick (remember to **replace** the stone carefully after you have finished your observations)
- on the surface of the soil or grass
- on the underside of different leaves growing on bushes or trees.

Observe at each location for 5 minutes. Take a hand lens or a magnifying glass with you if you have one.

On a piece of paper, write down what you see and where, and then record what you find in a table like the one below when you come back home.

Got the idea? Make sure you don't disturb small animals – just look closely.

Visit 1 to the garden/park   Date: ....

Where I looked for small animals	What I found
Under a large stone/brick	
On the surface of the grass/soil	
On the underside of leaves	

After your first visit answer questions 1–3.

1 In which place did you find the biggest variety of animals?

....

2 Which animal was there the most of?

....

This activity continues on the next page

12 KS2 ReviseWise Science

3 Did you find any evidence of animals that you did not actually see at the time, e.g. small holes eaten in leaves or slime trails?

....

Visit 2 to the garden/park   Date: ....

Where I looked for small animals	What I found
Under a large stone/brick	
On the surface of the grass/soil	
On the underside of leaves	

After your second visit, answer these questions.

Was there a difference in the weather on your two visits?

4 Which animals did you find in the same places on both visits?

....

5 Were there the same number and variety in each place? (Give examples.)

....

The following food chains include some small animals you may have observed.

Food chain 1:   rose bush   →   greenfly   →   ladybird
Food chain 2:   pansy   →   snail   →   thrush
Food chain 3:   rotting leaves →   woodlouse   →   centipede

6 Which animals in the food chains above are **predators**?

....

7 What is the scientific name given to the green plants at the start of a food chain?
.... Why is this?................................

....

Have you answered all the questions?

Microbes and decay

Wise up!

Learn these key points about microbes and decay.

- Remember, micro-organisms can be both helpful and harmful to people.
- Fungi (moulds) and bacteria can be helpful. For example, they prevent a build-up of waste by causing it to decay, e.g. in a compost heap. They are used in making yoghurt, beer and bread.
- Microbes can be harmful when they cause food to rot. They can cause infections in plants and animals.
- You can record your results in different ways, e.g. tables, drawings, graphs.

Activity

Read the sentences below and decide whether the microbes are **harmful** or **helpful** to humans.

Write either the word **harmful** or the word **helpful** on the line provided.

1 Microbes cause chicken pox. ....
2 Microbes cause leaves to rot. ....
3 Microbes cause bread to rise. ....
4 Microbes cause milk to change to yoghurt. ....
5 Microbes cause milk to turn sour. ....
6 Microbes cause the acid that makes teeth decay. ....

Ted and Sarah wanted to find out which conditions the microbes that cause bread to turn mouldy prefer.

A They put dry bread in a bag on the table.
B They put fresh bread in a bag on the table. The room was at 25°C.
C They put fresh bread in a bag in the fridge.
D They put stale, dry bread in a bag in the fridge. The fridge was at 4°C.

They drew the bread after one week to show what happened. Look at their pictures below.

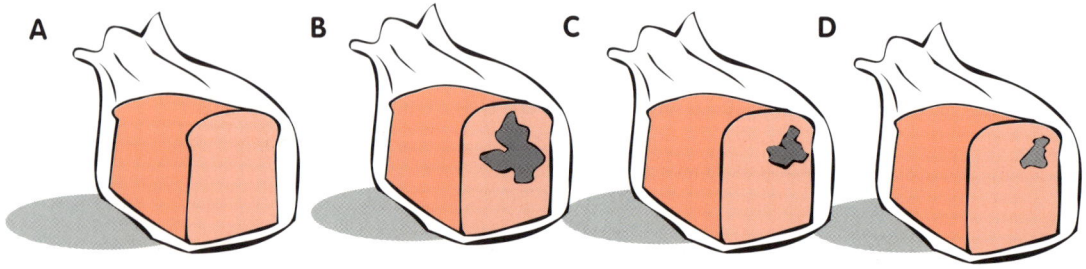

14 KS2 ReviseWise Science

This activity continues on the next page

7 Where did the mould grow best?

....

8 Explain why the mould grew better here.

....

9 Why was there more mould in Bag C than Bag D?

....

10 Use the results to explain why:

a) food is sometimes dried before it is packaged and sold, e.g. dried fruit

....

b) people store many foods in a fridge or freezer

....

Follow-up activity

Inside 3 separate clear plastic bags place a small piece of fruit or cheese. Seal the bags and place one in the fridge, one in the freezer and one in a room where you can see it easily.

Observe the changes that take place over a 2 week period.

1   Write down your prediction of what will happen. (Say how long you think it will be before you see any changes and what they might be.)

....

2   Make a table on which you can record your observations. (Decide how often you will record – every 2 days or every 5 days?) Give it an appropriate title.

When you have all your results, answer the following questions.

3   In which place did the microbes grow least well?

....

4   Where do think you could put a bag to cause the microbes to grow more? Explain why you have suggested this.

....

What do you know about teeth?

Wise up!

Make sure you know these things about teeth:

- humans have two sets of teeth during their life
- the names of different types of teeth
- teeth do various different things – they are used to bite, cut, tear and grind
- you can keep you teeth healthy by regular brushing after meals.

Activity

Complete this crossword to show what you know about human teeth.

Across

3 This substance is present in sweets and can help to cause tooth decay. (5)

5 Humans have this number of sets of teeth in a lifetime. (3)

6 This chemical is added to some water supplies and some toothpastes to help prevent tooth decay. (8)

7 These teeth are used to grind the food you eat. (6)

8 All teeth are used to do this. (4)

Down

1 These micro-organisms can help to cause tooth decay. (8)

2 When you have finished one of these you should brush your teeth. (4)

4 You must do this regularly to keep your teeth clean. (5)

6 You must eat a variety of this to keep your teeth and body healthy. (4)

16 KS2 ReviseWise Science

Human growth

> **Wise up!**
> To prepare for questions on human growth:
> - practise reading information from a graph
> - remember that you can record information on a graph or in a table
> - learn how to recognise patterns in data
> - understand that humans and almost all animals increase in size as they grow.

Activity

Jon plotted a graph to show how much his sister, Emily, weighed from birth to 60 days old.

1 What did Emily weigh when she was born?

....

2 After 80 days Emily weighed 4.5kg. Mark this correctly on the graph.

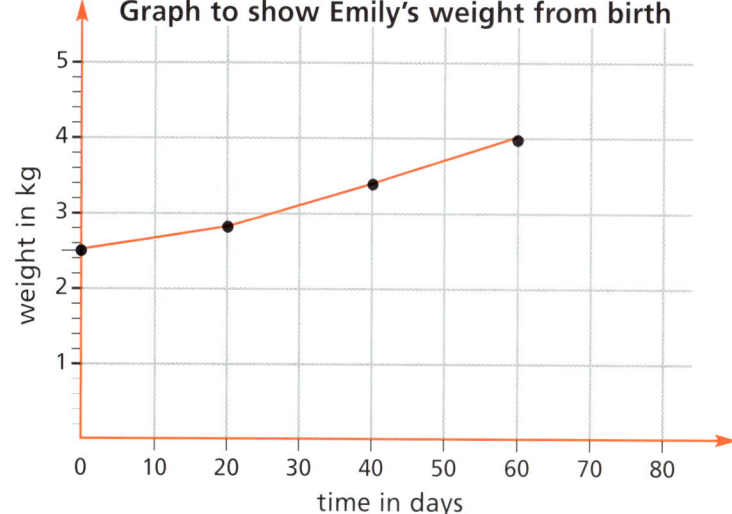

Emily is now in Year 6. Her friends all weigh themselves and record their results in this table. Look for Emily's name and mass.

Practise reading information from graphs and charts.

Name	Weight in kg
Susan	59
Josh	58
Emily	48
Tom	53

3 What does Emily weigh now that she is in Year 6?

....

4 There is evidence of one life process in the information shown on the graph and in the table. Which one is it?

....

Taking a pulse

Wise up!

Remember these points about pulse rates.
- Exercise causes pulse rate to increase.
- After exercise your pulse rate will eventually return to its resting rate.
- Pulse rates vary in children and adults.
- You can record information in a table.
- You can read information from a graph.

Activity

Measure your own pulse rate and that of an adult at rest. Do this by counting the number of beats in one minute. Then measure your own pulse rate after a variety of different activities e.g. after running up and down the stairs for a minute, sitting writing, and walking for a minute. Let your pulse rate go back to normal (your resting rate) before you start your next activity.

Activity	Pulse rate (in beats per minute)	
	You:	Adult:
1 At rest		
2		
3		
4		
5		

Record your results in this table. Don't forget to have a rest between each of your activities.

When you have completed your table, try answering these questions.

1 Are the resting pulse rates of the child and the adult identical? ....

2 Which activity caused your pulse rate to increase the most? ....

3 What is pulse rate a measure of? ....

4 Draw 4 lines to match the activities to the pulse rate listed below. Use each number only once.

a) While sitting   b) After sprinting   c) Just after waking up from a sleep   d) After 2 minutes of walking

Pulse rate

70	60	80	130

Ask an adult for help if you don't know how to take a pulse.

Drugs and health

Wise up!
Bear these things in mind:
- smoking can be harmful to health
- drugs and alcohol can also have harmful effects.

Activity

Smoking causes fatal diseases.

Smoking causes lung cancer.

Smoking causes heart disease.

Smoking when pregnant harms your baby.

Smoking kills.

Protect children. Don't make them breathe your smoke.

Look at these warnings that can be found on cigarette packets.

1 Write down 4 **different** ways in which smoking can be harmful to human health.

a) ....

b) ....

c) ....

d) ....

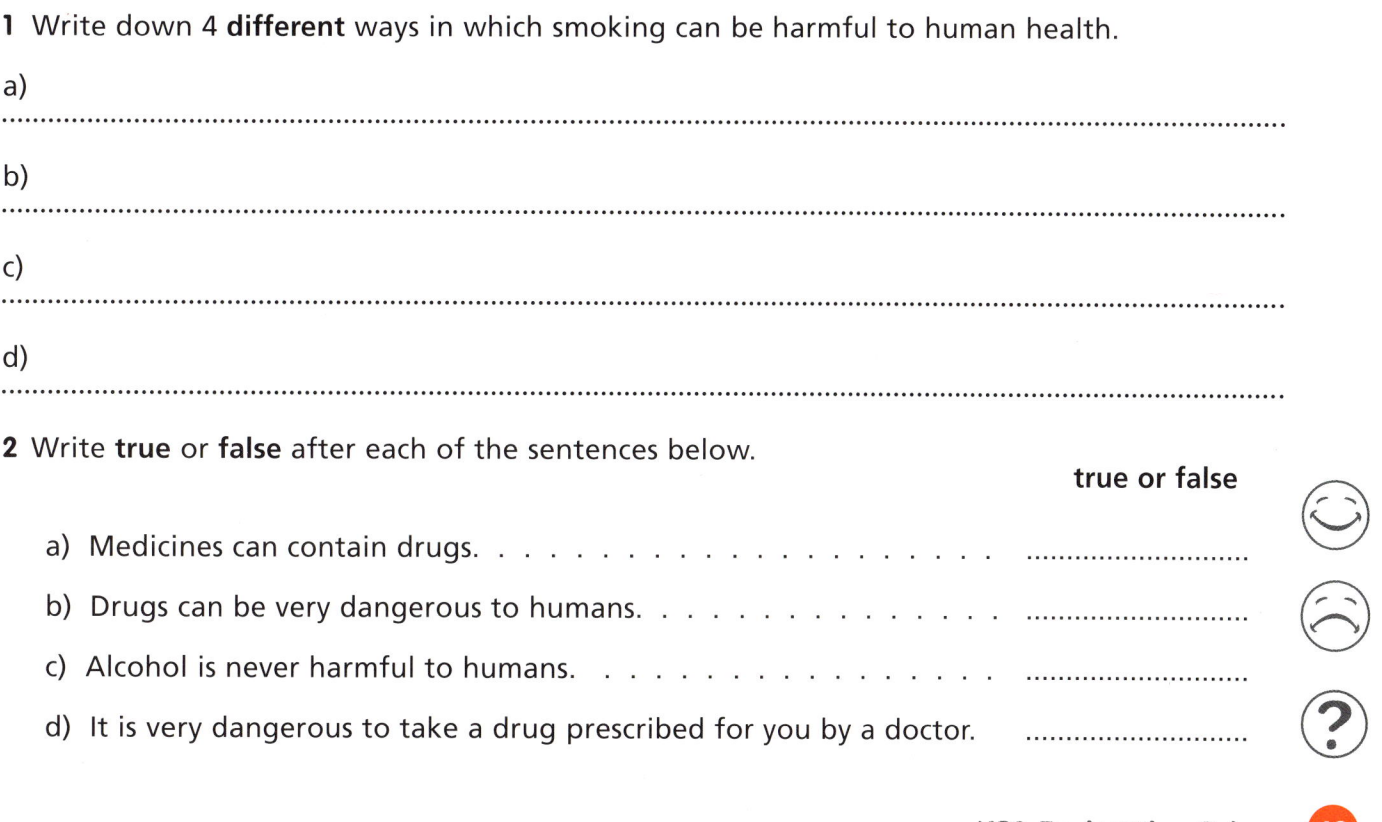

2 Write **true** or **false** after each of the sentences below.

                                                                                        true or false

a) Medicines can contain drugs. . . . .

b) Drugs can be very dangerous to humans. . . . .

c) Alcohol is never harmful to humans. . . . .

d) It is very dangerous to take a drug prescribed for you by a doctor. ....

Growing plants from seed

Wise up!

These facts will help you answer questions on growing plants from seed.

- Seeds are produced by plants so that more of the same plants will grow in the future.
- Seeds are dispersed (spread from the parent plant) by wind, water, animal and explosion.
- All seeds need water to germinate (start to grow).
- Roots grow first, taking in water, then the shoots grow.
- Green plants make their own food, from carbon dioxide (in the air) and water, using sunlight absorbed by the leaves.
- If green plants don't have any light, they will die.

Activity

You have probably seen a variety of plants grow and develop. Have you ever tried to grow you own plants from seed?

Choose 3 different types of seed to grow. Some that germinate and grow quickly are radish, pea, bean, carrot, tomato, dandelion.

Put about 10 seeds in a dish with damp paper towel in the bottom. Put the dish inside a polythene bag and seal it. Then put it in a warm place so that the seeds stay moist and germinate quickly. (If you want, you can put another dish in a cold place, such as a fridge, to see how temperature affects the rate at which the seeds germinate.)

Record what you see happening by drawing and completing a table like the one below. You may wish to leave larger spaces for writing what you see.

Name of seed	Day 1	Day 2	Day 3	Day 4	Day 5	Day 6	Day 7

After one week, try to answer these questions.

1 Did the roots grow first on all of your seeds? ....

2 Which type of seed germinated most quickly? ....

3 On which day did you see the first leaves on your seedlings? ....

4 Why do your seedlings need light once they have germinated? (You can try putting them in a dark place, still giving them water, to see what happens.)

....

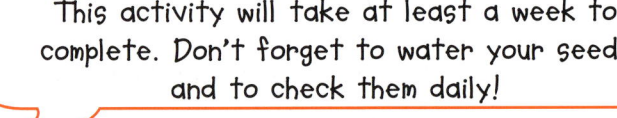

This activity will take at least a week to complete. Don't forget to water your seeds and to check them daily!

Variety in plants

Wise up!

Learn these key points about variety in plants.
- Remember, there are many types of plants.
- Humans eat various parts of plants.
- The different parts of a plant have different functions (they do different things).
- Plants grow at different rates.
- Green plants provide the food for all animals, either directly or indirectly.
- You can read information on a graph.

Activity

Look at the wide range of plants growing in your house, around school or in gardens and parks. Look carefully at the different leaves, flowers, stems and roots to see the similarities and differences.

1 Match the name of the plant to the part that we eat by drawing a line.

    a) lettuce   i) seed
    b) carrot   ii) stem
    c) celery   iii) leaf
    d) apple   iv) root
    e) hazelnut   v) fruit

Can you think of other plants that we eat the fruit from?

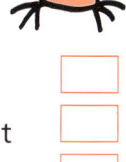

2 The root of a plant is important for several reasons.
Tick the **THREE** correct reasons in the list below.

it anchors the plant ☐	it makes food for the plant ☐
it holds the plant upright ☐	it takes in nutrients for the plant ☐
it takes in water for the plant ☐	it takes in light for the plant ☐

3 Explain why leaves are important to plants.

....

....

4 Some flowers are brightly coloured and scented. Why?

....

....

This activity continues on the next page

21

5 Some children measured two plants in their classroom. The plants were the same type, but were kept in different places. They recorded the increase in height every 4 days over 2 weeks.

They plotted a graph of their findings (see right).

Look at the graph and then answer the questions below.

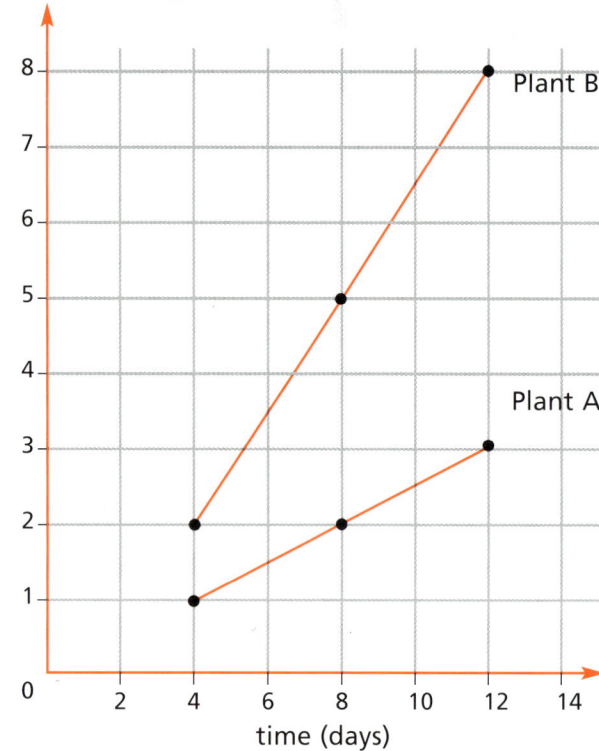

Graph to show the increase in height of Plant A and Plant B

a) What height was Plant A after 5 days?

.... cm

b) Which plant grew the most over the two weeks?

....

c) Explain how the graph shows you which plant grew faster.

....

d) Give one reason why the two plants grew at different rates.

....

Follow-up activity

Measure the increase in height of two different plants growing in your house or garden over a two week period. Record your measurements either as a table or as a graph like the one above.

Have you answered all the questions?

Classifying materials

Wise up!

This information will help you classify materials.

- Objects can be made from different materials.
- Materials have different properties, such as hardness, strength, flexibility, and absorbency.
- The material used to make a particular object depends on its properties.

Activity

1. Collect 6 different objects. Look carefully at each one and complete the chart by writing down what material it is made from and why you think it is made from that particular material. An example has been done for you.

Name of object	Name of material and why is this material used?
paperclip	metal (steel). It is strong and stiff (rigid), but can be bent to make the right shape.
i)	
ii)	
iii)	
iv)	
v)	
vi)	

2. Put a ring around the objects that are made from a rigid material:

   polythene bag   wooden pencil   paper book   plastic pen   woollen scarf

3. Put a ring around the objects that are usually made from metal:

   key   ring   book   table   mug   saucepan

4. Explain why metal is a good material to use to make these objects.

   ....

Why not draw another table on a piece of paper and try sorting some more objects?

Investigating magnetism and electricity

> **Wise up!**
> Try to learn the following facts about magnetism and electricity.
> - Not all metals are magnetic.
> - All metals conduct electricity.
> - There are forces that pull together (attract) and push away (repel) between magnets.

Activity

Look around your home and at your toys. See if you can find any magnets being used, e.g. in some train sets, travel games, cupboard doors, fridge decorations. When you find some, look carefully to see exactly how and why they work.

1 Read the following sentences. Write **true** or **false** after each.

When magnetism is used to keep two things together, the two items must be made from:

True or false

a) two magnetic metals

b) one magnet and one magnetic metal

c) one magnet and one non-magnetic metal

d) two magnets with their unlike poles together

e) two magnets with their like poles together

2 Tim made a collection of objects.

Put a tick ✓ if the material is magnetic (attracted to a magnet) or a cross ✗ if it isn't.

Object	Magnetic? ✓ or ✗	Object	Magnetic? ✓ or ✗
gold ring		wooden pencil	
aluminium foil		iron nail	
plastic spoon		copper bracelet	
steel knife		silver medal	
steel can		paper cup	

3 Put a ring around the materials that are both magnetic **and** conduct electricity.

copper   plastic   pencil "lead" (graphite)   steel   gold

iron   wood   silver   glass   nylon

Think carefully before you answer the questions. Use the Wise up box to help you!

Solids, liquids and gases

Wise up!

Keep in mind these facts.
- All substances exist as a solid, liquid or gas at room temperature.
- Substances can change from solid to liquid or liquid to gas and back again.
- **Melting** is when a solid changes to a liquid.
- **Evaporation** is when a liquid changes to a gas.
- **Condensation** is when a gas changes to a liquid.
- Water in its solid form is called ice and in its gas form is called water vapour.

Activity

1. On a separate piece of paper make a list of different solids, liquids and gases you can find in your home. Try to list 10 solids, 10 liquids and 2 gases. Look out for unusual mixtures, e.g. foam, which is a liquid with gas in it.

2. Find the answers to the clues a)–j). The words can be found in the wordsearch below. The answers go forwards, backwards and diagonally across the wordsearch.

   a) The name of the gas made when liquid water changes. (5,6) ....
   b) The name of the process when solid changes to liquid. (7) ....
   c) The name of a very light gas sometimes used in party balloons. (6) ....
   d) The name of the liquid formed when ice is heated. (5) ....
   e) The name of the process when gas changes to liquid. (12) ....
   f) The name for any substance that keeps its shape. (5) ....
   g) The name for a substance that takes the shape of the container it's in. (6) ....

Work out the answer and write it next to the clue. Then, try to find the words in the grid.

M	H	E	Y	A	O	M	A	N	C	R	V
E	E	L	G	E	E	T	W	U	M	P	S
L	W	V	B	T	R	I	A	X	D	M	E
T	Y	K	A	I	T	T	T	C	L	W	S
I	A	L	I	P	Y	O	E	I	I	D	A
N	S	Q	U	R	O	P	R	J	Q	I	G
G	K	O	V	O	H	R	V	W	U	L	O
C	O	N	D	E	N	S	A	T	I	O	N
A	W	P	L	E	A	T	P	T	D	S	E
A	R	I	E	T	E	Q	O	K	I	T	Y
N	U	T	Z	R	U	Z	U	V	L	O	M
M	E	A	C	C	I	A	R	B	E	U	N

h) This group of materials are almost all solid at room temperature and conduct electricity. (5) ....
i) The name of the process when liquid changes to gas. (11) ....
j) Air is a mixture of these. (5) ....

Evaporation in everyday life

Wise up!

Learn these key points about evaporation.
- The process by which a liquid changes to a gas is called evaporation.
- Liquid water changes into a gas called water vapour.
- Water will evaporate slowly at low temperatures and more quickly at higher temperatures.
- You can recognise patterns in data.

Activity

On a dry day, make a puddle of water by pouring 100cm³ on a level area of concrete or stone in your garden or on the pavement outside your home.

Watch how it spreads out by flowing over the surface. This is a property of all liquids. Look at the puddle every half hour to see how long it takes to disappear.

1 Estimate how long it will take for the puddle to disappear ....

2 What happens to the water when the puddle disappears? ....

3 What happens to the rate at which a puddle disappears if it is a very hot day?

....

Tim and Alex wanted to see how long 3 identical face flannels would take to dry. They made each flannel damp with water, then weighed them. Each weighed 35g. They put one on a hot radiator, one in a warm room and one in a cool room. They weighed them each hour and plotted a graph of their results.

4 Where had the children placed the face flannel that weighed 30g after 2 hours?

....

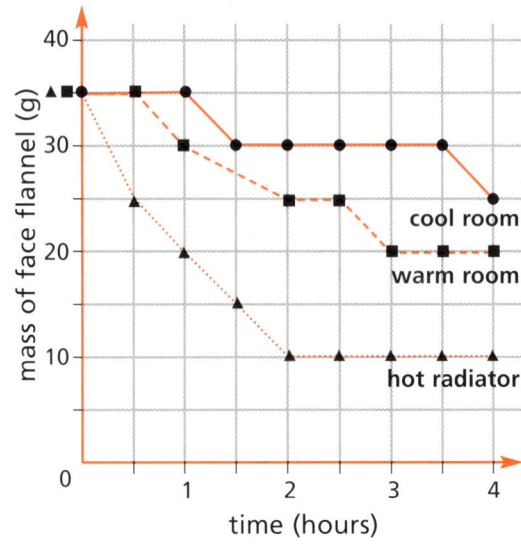

 5 In which place did the water evaporate most slowly?

....

 6 What was the mass of the dry face flannel? How do you know?

....

26 KS2 ReviseWise Science

Making a solution

Wise up!

You should be aware that:
- some solids dissolve in water to give a solution
- dissolving is an example of a change that can be reversed (undone)
- when the liquid of a solution evaporates, the solid that dissolved is left behind
- some changes cannot be reversed (irreversible), e.g. burning.

Activity

1 Try mixing one teaspoonful of each substance in the table below into a glass of cold water (about 100cm^3), one at a time. Use fresh water each time. Use a clear glass so that you can see the changes easily. Stir for about one minute, watching carefully to see if all the solid dissolves, some of the solid dissolves or none of the solid dissolves. Write your observations in the table below. Repeat your tests using warm water.

Name of substance	Cold water observations	Warm water observations
a) sugar		
b) salt		
c) chalk		
d) wax		
e) tea-leaves		
f) bicarbonate of soda		

Place a small amount (a few drops) of sugar solution on a clean, clear piece of plastic. Leave the plastic on a window sill in a warm room.

2 What can you see on the plastic after a few hours?

....

3 What has happened to the water? Where has it gone?

....

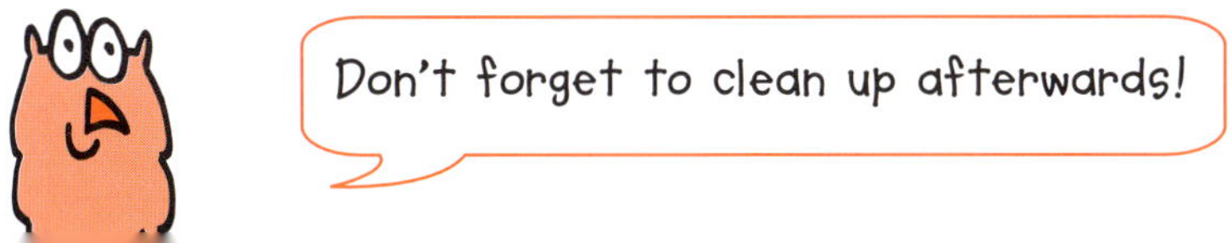

Reversible / irreversible changes

Wise up!

Remember these key points.
- Some changes can be undone (reversed) and others cannot.
- Melting and dissolving are both reversible changes.
- **Melting** is the process when a solid changes to a liquid.
- **Dissolving** is when a solid mixes with a liquid forming a clear solution.

Activity

Write the word **melting** or **dissolving** after each of the sentences below.

Melting or dissolving

1. Solid wax changing to liquid wax. ....
2. Sugar mixing with water. ....
3. Ice changing to water. ....
4. Instant coffee granules mixing with hot water. ....
5. Jelly mixing with hot water. ....
6. Chocolate becoming soft and runny. ....
7. Gold being heated and poured into moulds. ....
8. A snowman disappearing. ....

Tick the boxes which show a **reversible** change.

9. Candle wax burning. ☐
10. Candle wax melting. ☐
11. Bread being heated to toast. ☐
12. Margarine being heated to melt. ☐
13. Water changing to water vapour. ☐
14. Wood changing to charcoal. ☐
15. Water changing to ice. ☐

This is quite hard. Look for the key words in the sentences which can help you to answer correctly.

Separating a mixture

Wise up!

When answering questions on separating a mixture, don't forget that:

- substances can be separated using different methods
- sieving, filtering and evaporating are all methods of separating substances
- sieving and filtering can be used to separate substances that do not dissolve in water.

Activity

1 Joe has made a mess. By mistake he has mixed up sand, iron filings, sugar and water. Put a ring around the equipment he needs to use to separate the substances.

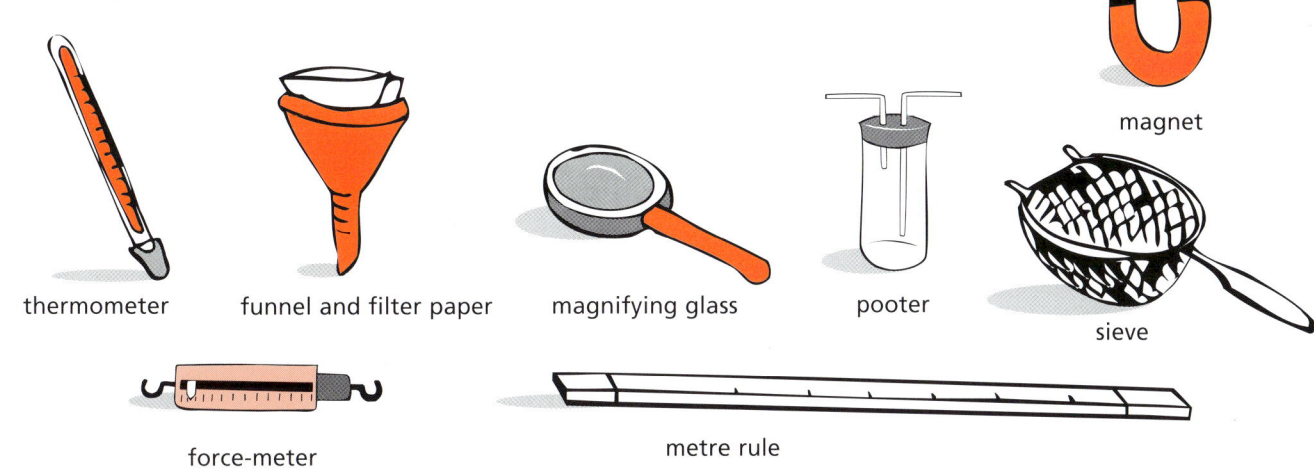

thermometer   funnel and filter paper   magnifying glass   pooter   magnet   sieve

force-meter   metre rule

2 Describe the 3 steps Joe should take to separate the 3 solids.

a) **Step 1** First he should

....

....

b) **Step 2** Next he should

....

....

c) **Step 3** Then he should

....

....

Wise up to the help at the top of the page!

Electricity – symbols

Wise up!

You'll be able to draw a good circuit diagram if you remember:

- that symbols are used to represent electrical components
- which symbol represents which component
- that there should be no gaps at all in a circuit diagram because a gap means that the circuit is not complete and therefore the electricity will not flow.

Activity

Complete the sentences below by writing the word or drawing the symbol.

1. ⊗ is the symbol for a ....

2. ⊻ is the symbol for a ....

3. ⊦⊢ is the symbol for a ....

4. .... is the symbol for a motor.

5. .... is the symbol for a switch.

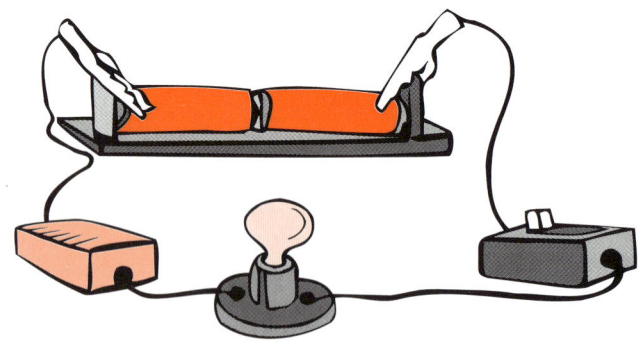

David makes a circuit using

2 cells (batteries), a switch,
a bulb and a buzzer, like this:

6 Use the correct symbols to draw David's circuit here:

In the Test you will always be given the symbols, so this is a hard question!

30 KS2 ReviseWise Science

Looking at switches

Wise up!

Learn these facts about switches.
- Electrical devices have a switch to turn them on and off.
- A switch is a way of making and breaking a circuit.
- When a switch is in the off position it prevents the electricity from flowing through by creating a gap in the circuit.

Activity

Look carefully at these drawings of two different switches. They are shown in the **OFF** position and in the **ON** position.

A press switch

OFF

A toggle switch

Arm doesn't touch metal tab.

metal tab.

ON

Arm moves down to touch metal tab.

metal tab.

1 Describe what happens when the switch is turned on.

a) The press switch: ....

....

b) The toggle switch: ....

....

2 Explain why a bulb in a circuit lights up when the switch is turned on.

....

....

Remember to look for key information in the Wise up! box.

KS2 ReviseWise Science **31**

Looking at friction

Wise up!

To answer questions about friction, you need to know that:
- friction is a force that opposes movement
- a smoother surface gives less resistance (friction) to movement than a rough one
- objects slow down and stop more quickly on a rough surface
- forces can be measured.

Activity

Try pushing and letting go of a coin or other small object across different surfaces, e.g. the floor, a carpet, a polished table. Note on which surface it moves most easily.

1 Describe the force that starts your object moving.

....

2 Name the force that causes the object to stop moving.

....

Nick and Vincent measure how far a 10p coin slides on a table when they push it. They try pushing it harder and more gently. They polish their table, then try their test again.

Look at the table below.

	\multicolumn{6}{c}{distance travelled}
Size of force	\multicolumn{3}{c}{Table top}	\multicolumn{3}{c}{Polished table top}
	1st try	2nd try	3rd try	1st try	2nd try	3rd try
Gentle push	5cm	8cm	4cm	12cm	15cm	20cm
Medium push	10cm	17cm	10cm	50cm	45cm	60cm
Hard push	15cm	21cm	34cm	70cm	105cm	75cm

3 On which surface did the coin travel furthest? Explain how you know this.

....

....

4 Describe how the size of the force affects the distance the coin moves.

....

....

Got the idea? Now test yourself by doing the crossword on the next page.

32 KS2 ReviseWise Science

Know your forces

Wise up!

To understand forces, remember:
- forces act in particular directions
- forces can be measured
- why some forces have special names.

Activity

Across

1 When two forces are equal we say they are .... (8)
4 The piece of equipment used to measure forces. (10)
6 We measure the .... of a force in units shown as N. (4)
7 The name of the force that will push upwards on an object put in water. (8)
8 The pull of gravity always acts in this direction. (4)
9 The unit used to measure force. (6)

Down

2 The name of the force that slows objects moving through air. (3,10)
3 The name of the force of attraction between an object and the Earth. (7)
4 A push, a pull and a twist are all examples of this. (5)
5 The name of the force that slows any moving object. (8)

Complete this crossword using the clues on the right.

Investigating forces

> **Wise up!**
>
> When investigating forces, remember the following:
> - when a spring is pressed down, you can feel an opposing push back
> - when a floating object is pushed down in water, you can feel an opposing push upwards
> - on Earth, 100g mass usually exerts a force of one Newton, 1N.

Activity

In a sink full of water, try pressing down on some floating objects, e.g. a plastic bottle with its lid on, a ball, an apple, an inflated balloon.

1 Describe how difficult it is to push the different objects under the water.

....

2 What happens when you stop pushing on a floating object? Explain this in term of forces.

....

....

Some children have weighed themselves. They have entered their weights in the table on the right.

3 Complete their table by entering the force (in Newtons) that they are exerting on the ground. You need to know that 1kg exerts a force of 10N.

Name	Mass in kg	Force in N
Gary	32	
Jessica	38	
Darren	21	
Arun	30	
Sophie	25	

Samina pressed down on a large spring. She noticed that it squashed to a smaller length. When she pressed harder it became shorter.

The harder I press the spring, the shorter it becomes.

She has correctly identified the relationship between **TWO** factors.

4 Name the **TWO** factors.

a) .... and b) ....

Pushing and pulling

Wise up!

Remember these things about forces that push and pull.

- Don't forget that forces can act in different directions.
- When objects are pushed or pulled, an opposing force can be felt.
- Objects are pulled downwards because of the gravitational attraction between them and the Earth.

Activity

Underneath the drawings, write down what the forces are and state the direction in which they are acting. The first one has been done for you.

1 Hand pushing down on ball and upthrust of water pushing up on the ball.

2 ....

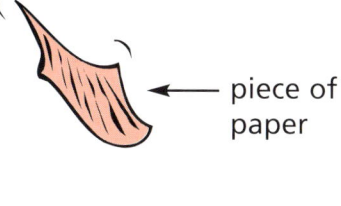

piece of paper

sponge

3 ....

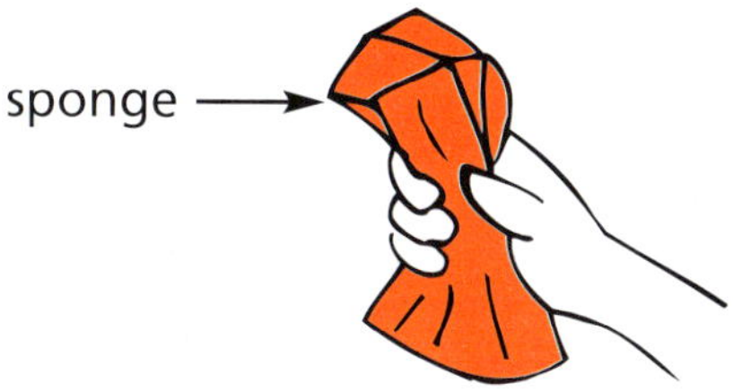

4 ....

Suzy makes a model see-saw. One side goes down when she puts a 100g mass on it.

5 What must she do to make the right-hand side go down to the ground?

....

How did you do? Remember to use Wise up! boxes on this and other pages to help you.

Investigating light

Wise up!

Make sure you know these key points about light.

- Light travels from a source.
- The Sun is the Earth's main source of light during daylight hours.
- Light is reflected from surfaces. Some surfaces reflect light better than others, e.g. a mirror.
- Some objects look bright or shiny because they reflect light from their surfaces well.
- You see objects when light reflected from them enters your eyes.

Activity

Some objects give out light. Some reflect light.

1 Draw a circle around the objects below that are a **source of light** (give out light).

torch	mirror	plastic bottle	candle	Moon
Sun	lamp-post	aluminium foil	car headlamp	firework
window	metal spoon	silver cup	computer screen	

2 Josh can see a book on the table behind him by looking in his mirror.
   Which sentence best explains why.
   Tick **ONE** box.
   The mirror reflects light which enters Josh's eyes.
   The Sun is shining on the mirror.
   The mirror is a source of light and the light enters Josh's eyes.
   Josh can't see the mirror if it's dark.
   Josh's eyes give out light which reflects back from the mirror.

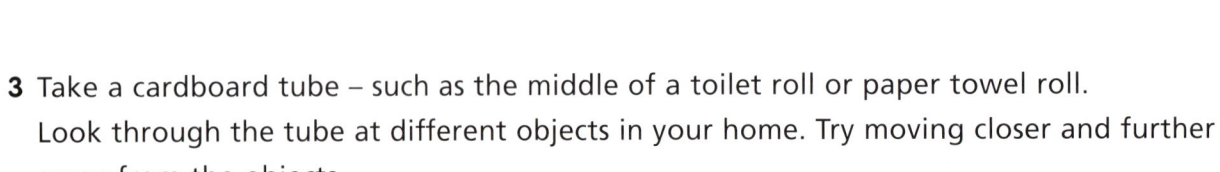

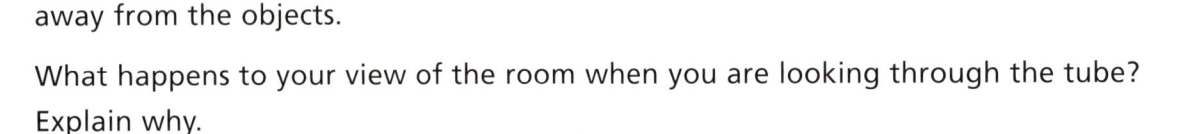

3 Take a cardboard tube – such as the middle of a toilet roll or paper towel roll.
   Look through the tube at different objects in your home. Try moving closer and further away from the objects.

   What happens to your view of the room when you are looking through the tube?
   Explain why.

A closer look at light

Wise up!

Learning these terms and facts will be useful for answering questions about light.

- Light can pass through some materials and not others.
- An **opaque** material blocks the light.
- A **translucent** material lets some light pass through.
- A **transparent** material lets light pass through without distortion.
- When light is blocked by an object, a shadow forms.

Activity

On a sunny day, go outside and observe the size and shape of the shadows made by your body (or parts of your body, e.g. your hand near a wall) and those of some other opaque objects. Or, use a torch as your light source and explore the shadows made by holding your hand and other opaque objects between the torch and the wall.

1 Describe the difference between the shadows made when an object is close to the surface on which the shadow is being created and those made when it is far away. Explain why this is.

....

....

2 Amit and Graham shine a torch at some different objects.
   Write down whether you think the objects are **opaque**, **translucent** or **transparent**.

   a) mirror ....
   b) wine glass ....
   c) book ....
   d) tissue paper ....

   e) cellophane sweet wrapper ....
   f) compact disc ....
   g) nylon curtains ....
   h) aluminium foil ....

3 They notice that all the opaque objects make a very dark shadow. Why is this?

....

4 Some objects make a faint shadow. Why is this?

....

Phew! That was hard!

Making noise

Wise up!

Remember these facts about sound.

- Sounds are made when objects vibrate. You cannot always see the vibrations that create a sound.
- The pitch of a sound can be changed.
- A short length of wire, or column of air, will produce a higher note than a longer one.
- A tighter drum skin will produce a higher note than a looser one.

Activity

Stretch a piece of clingfilm over a dish so that it makes a tight surface. Place about 10 grains of rice on the tight cling film. Now take a metal baking tray and hold it about 5cm above the cling film. Hit the baking tray with a wooden spoon so that it makes a loud sound. Watch the rice. You should be able to see it move. It will "jump" higher, the louder the noise made when you hit the baking tray.

1 Explain why the rice moves when you hit the baking tray.

....

2 What does the sound travel through to reach the cling film? ....

3 You can also feel a tingling in the hand that is holding the baking tray when you hit it. Why is this?

....

Look at these drawings of musical instruments. They are drawn to scale. They all make a sound when a column of air vibrates.

Look carefully at the size of the instruments.

A flute   **B** bassoon   **C** clarinet   **D** saxophone   **E** piccolo

4 Write the names of the instruments in order, from the one that can make the highest-pitched note to the one that can make the lowest-pitched note.

....

Why can't you hear any noise in space?

38 KS2 ReviseWise Science

Good vibrations

Wise up!

Look carefully at these points about sound and vibration.

- A louder sound can be heard over a longer distance.
- Vibrations from sound sources require a medium to travel through, e.g. air, wood, metal.
- You cannot always see the vibrations from a sound source.
- You can use results to compare information.

Activity

Ravi and Natalie want to find out how far away their friend Tom can hear sounds. Ravi hits 2 pencils together, with the same force each time, to make a sound.
Natalie drops a pin onto a book from the same height each time, to make a sound. They record their results in the table below.

Answer the questions below using the information in the table.

Tom's distance from sound source (m)	Pencil being hit together	Pin dropped onto book
5	Yes	Yes
10	Yes	No
15	Yes, very faintly	No
20	No	No

1 Could Tom hear both sounds equally at all distances? Explain how you know this.

....

....

2 Describe how the **distance** from which you can hear a sound depends on the **loudness** of the sound.

....

....

KS2 ReviseWise Science 39

The Earth in space

Wise up!

Look at these facts about the Earth in space.

- The position of the Sun appears to change in the sky during the day.
- The shadow of an object changes when its position changes relative to the source of light.
- Day (periods of light) and night (periods of darkness) occur because the Earth rotates on its axis.
- When half of the Earth's surface is receiving light from the Sun, the other half is in darkness.

Activity

1. Look at the drawing on the right.

   Which is the correct shadow when the Sun appears overhead? Tick **ONE** box.

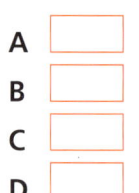

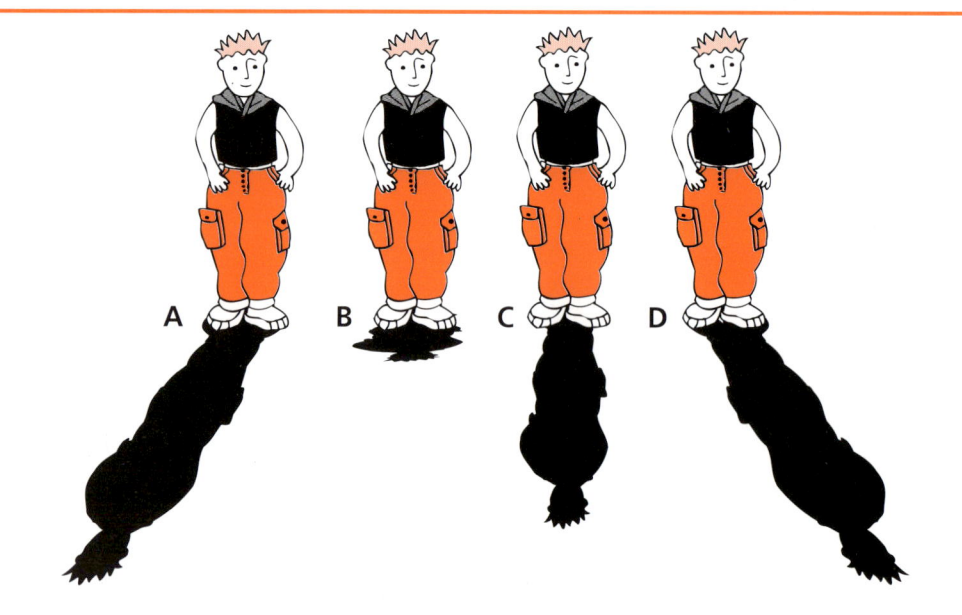

   A ☐
   B ☐
   C ☐
   D ☐

2. John shines a torch onto a ball. The torch represents the Sun and the ball represents the Earth. Match the labels to the letters on the drawing below:

   | Sun | Earth | day time |
   | light from Sun | night time |

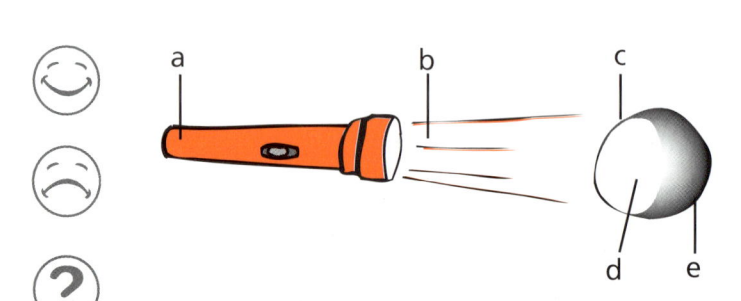

3. A **mnemonic** is a sentence or rhyme that can help you remember particular things in order. Each word of the sentence begins with a letter of the words you are trying to remember.

   For example, the order of the planets is: **M**ercury, **V**enus, **E**arth, **M**ars, **J**upiter, **S**aturn, **U**ranus, **N**eptune and **P**luto.

   For fun, try making up a mnemonic to help you remember the correct order of the planets from the Sun.

   An example is:
   My **V**ery **E**arly **M**orning **J**am **S**andwiches **U**sually **N**auseate **P**eople.

Use the information at the top of the page to help you remember the facts.

40 KS2 ReviseWise Science

Sun, Earth and Moon

Wise up!

You need to know that:
- the Earth takes one year (365.25 days) to orbit (move around) the Sun
- the moon orbits the Earth approximately every 28 days
- the Earth spins on its axis once every 24 hours
- the Sun, Earth and moon are all approximately spherical (round).

Activity

Natalie, Ravi and Tom are talking about the Earth, Sun and Moon.

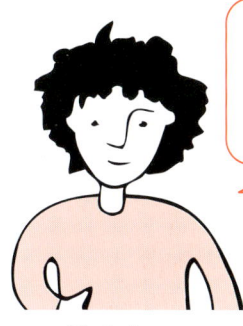

Natalie: *The Earth moves around the Moon and the Sun.*

Ravi: *The Earth moves around the Sun.*

Tom: *The Sun moves around the Earth.*

1 Who is correct? ....

2 Explain why the Sun appears to move in the sky during the course of a day.

....

....

3 How long does it take for the moon to orbit the Earth? ....

4 Which movement of the Earth takes 24 hours?

....

5 Match the words on the left to the correct phrase on the right by drawing a line linking the two.

   a) orbit   i) to spin on an axis.
   b) day   ii) time taken for Earth to compete one turn on its axis.
   c) moon   iii) time taken for Earth to move around the Sun.
   d) rotate   iv) a spherical satellite of the Earth.
   e) year   v) to move in an approximately circular path around an object.

Remember to take time to read the questions carefully.

KS2 ReviseWise Science **41**

Answers to activities and guidance

This section is mainly for parents, to help them mark their child's answers. There are also some details that may help with the science background. The level the question is pitched at is shown, too. However, it's important to realise that the level pupils achieve is about their **overall** performance, so the level for each question should be used only as a guide. These levels are only one professional's interpretation of the level descriptors of the National Curriculum.

Using clues on the page (page 6–7)

1 Clues: **TWO** in bold type, 2 spaces to write on, the word 'and' indicates **how much** to write; Dotted lines and pencil show **where** to write.
Clematis and maple. By looking carefully at the diagrams, your child can see that both the clematis and maple have attachments to the seeds that help them fly with the wind, and so the seeds get spread further away from the parent plant. Knowledge of seed dispersal is Level 4.

2 Clues: pencil shows **where** to write, 6 lines show you that your child must write a full explanation.
Gravity is pulling both pieces of paper to the ground and air is pushing up against both pieces of paper as they fall. The smaller piece of paper has a smaller surface area so less air resistance acts on it. It will fall faster than a larger piece of paper. Explanation of forces acting on a falling object is indicative of Level 5.

3 Clues: pencil shows **where** to write, one line shows that only a **short** answer is needed. 10 days. Reading from a graph accurately requires awareness of the scale and the labels for each axis of the graph. A straight read-off like this is indicative of Level 3.

4 Clues: **TWO** in bold, two lines and the word 'and' show the need to give two words. Heart and lungs. If an answer asks for two names like this it usually requires both to be correct for one mark. In the test paper, your child can look at the boxes in the grey margin to see whether there are one or two boxes i.e. one or two marks awarded. Knowing about major body organs is Level 4.

5 Clues: one line shows that a short sentence is needed for the answer. They are not magnetic materials. Knowing that some materials are magnetic is indicative of Level 3, but knowing the names of specific magnetic and non-magnetic materials indicates Level 4.

6 Clues: **ONE** in bold indicates that your child must tick only one box. Wax. Knowing that some materials melt and others do not indicates Level 3.

Spot the mistakes (page 8–9)

1 The child has ticked **three** boxes instead of two as asked for. If this were a one-mark question, no marks would be gained. As it is a two-mark question, and the child has 2 correct and one wrong answer, one mark is gained. Correct answer: it melts; it becomes a liquid.

2 The answer given has tried to **explain** what happens, and does not give the **one word** description asked for – evaporation.

3 The child has written a producer (cabbage) and a consumer (caterpillar) and therefore will get no marks, as a right answer is cancelled by a wrong answer. Correct answer: cabbage OR grass

4 The child has not written Yes or No as asked for. However, markers will give credit where possible for a clear indication of what was intended e.g. a cross for No, but in this case the child would get one mark because all the No answers are correct, but the Yes are still not correct because of the "might be". (Should read Yes, No, Yes, No, Yes.)

5 a) 2 marks b) 1 mark c) 1 mark d) 2 marks

6 Because there are that number of marks in the boxes alongside the questions.

7 Give a reason why something happened – ticked

8 a) an account in words about a subject.
b) look for similarities and differences.
c) put in all the necessary parts or steps.

Answering questions (page 10–11)

1 Nutrition or feeding.

2 Snail.

3 It eats nuts, seeds, fruit and insects.

4 Prey. Answering all 4 questions correctly is indicative

42 KS2 ReviseWise Science

of Level 3, although knowing about the relationships in a food chain and using terms like predator and prey are indicative of Level 4.

5 The height of the slope. Being able to vary one factor at a time in a fair test is indicative of Level 4.

6 They thought it would make the ball go further. Recognising the prediction of the children is indicative of Level 3.

7 To check their results/make their results more accurate, because, for example, the ball may not have travelled in a straight line each time, making it difficult to measure. Knowing how and why to carry out a fair test is indicative of Level 4.

8 Because they had started with a tennis ball and so for the whole of their test they must keep this factor the same. Knowing that they must only vary one factor at a time, in this case the height of the ramp, is indicative of Level 4.

Researching habitats (page 12–13)

1 One mark for reading information correctly from the recording table – likely to be either under the stone or on the grass/soil. Being able to record observations on a table and read information from it is indicative of Level 3.

2 Possibly something like woodlice or ants under a stone but correct information should be read from the table of results.

3 Children may see eggs of small animals, "lines" on leaves where an insect larva has burrowed, "cuckoo spit" on some plants where the larva of frog hoppers are inside.

4 & 5 Looking for patterns in data of this type would be indicative of Level 4.

6 Answer requires understanding of the term predator i.e. an animal that feeds off another animal. Recognition of any of the animals at the end of the food chain – ladybird, thrush, centipede as predators (with greenfly, snail, woodlouse as their prey).

7 Producer. All green plants produce food from carbon dioxide and water, rather than feeding off other plants or animals. (The Sun is the source of energy for the food production in green plants.)

Microbes and decay (page 14–15)

1 Harmful **2** Helpful **3** Helpful
4 Helpful **5** Harmful **6** Harmful.

Knowledge of micro-organisms that can be helpful or harmful to humans is indicative of Level 3.

7 B, in the room where it was warm (and with the fresh bread which contains a lot of water).

8 Micro-organisms grow best in warm (and damp) conditions.

9 Because the fresh bread had more moisture than the stale dry bread.

10 a) Reducing the amount of water in food reduces the growth rate of microbes.

b) Reducing the temperature at which food is stored slows down the growth rate of microbes. Knowledge of the conditions under which microbes will grow is indicative of Level 4/5.

Follow-up activity

1 A answer that takes into account knowledge of microbes not growing well in cold places would gain marks. Being able to make predictions based on scientific knowledge indicates Level 3/4.

2 Being able to make and keep a table of results with a correct title, i.e. to show the growth of microbes in varying conditions, and select an appropriate recording interval is indicative of Level 4.

3 This is a simple reading from the results table – Level 3.

4 Name a warmer place (but may include knowledge that very hot conditions/boiling may kill microbes). Microbes prefer a warm, damp place.

What do you know about teeth? (page 16)

Across **3** sugar **5** two **6** fluoride **7** molars **8** bite
Down **1** bacteria **2** meal **4** brush **6** food

Human growth (page 17)

1 2.5kg. In this case the units (kg) are not given on the answer line. This shows that the correct units are required and a mark will not usually be given unless it is written. A read off answer from a graph like this indicates Level 3, though having to add units sometimes takes it to Level 4.

KS2 ReviseWise Science 43

2 The point should be clearly plotted with a neat cross at the point where the 80 day vertical line crosses the 4.5kg horizontal line.

3 48kg. Again units are required in the answer. Simple read-off from a table indicative of Level 3.

4 Growth. Knowledge that increase in mass/size is an indication of growth – one of the life processes that the children are expected to know about at Key Stage 2. Others include nutrition, movement, and reproduction, although they should know that getting rid of waste (excretion), sensing and respiration take place.

Taking a pulse (page 18)

1 Most children have a higher pulse rate than most adults. Being able to complete a given table correctly is indicative of Level 3.

2 The most strenuous activity chosen will have caused the pulse rate to increase most – i.e. running up and down stairs from the examples suggested. Reading correctly from a table is indicative of Level 3.

3 It is a measure of how fast the heart is beating in a given time, usually per minute.

4 Lines should join a) to 70, b) to 130, c) to 60, and d) to 80. Correct recognition of the effect of exercise on pulse rate is indicative of Level 4.

Drugs and health (page 19)

1a Smoking can cause lung cancer.
b Smoking can harm unborn children.
c Smoking causes heart disease.
d Smoking can kill you.

Using a secondary source of information like this is indicative of Level 3.

2 a) True b) True c) False d) False

To know the difference between drugs being helpful/harmful to humans in this format is indicative of Level 3.

Growing plants from seed (page 20)

1 Roots always grow first from seeds. Gaining this information correctly from the diary of results kept is indicative of Level 4.

2 Of the examples suggested, radish seeds usually germinate first, but it will depend on the type of seeds grown. The range depending on the different species, can be from one day to many months and even years in some cases! Reading this kind of information from the table is indicative of Level 3.

3 The appearance of leaves varies from one seedling to another. If radish seeds have been grown, the first leaves can usually be seen after about 4 days. Reading this kind of information from the table is indicative of Level 3.

4 All green plants need light to grow because light energy is used in the making of the food for the plant (by a process called photosynthesis). The light itself is not changed into food – it is the energy source used to combine the carbon dioxide and water taken in by the roots and leaves to make these into sugars.

Variety in plants (page 21)

1 Lines should connect the following words: a) to iii), b) to iv), c) to ii), d) to v), e) to i)

Knowing about basic parts of the plant like this would be indicative of Level 3.

2 Anchors the plant, takes in water for the plant and takes in nutrients for the plant all ticked. Knowledge of the function of roots is indicative of Level 5.

3 The leaves take in sunlight. They make the food for the plant. (They may also store water and nutrients on occasions but this would not necessarily be true of all green plants.) General, simple answers are expected. Knowledge of the functions of a leaf is indicative of Level 5 – more detailed answers about photosynthesis and gas exchange are not expected from primary children, although understanding of this would indicate Level 5/6.

4 To attract insects for pollination. Knowledge of the function of parts of a plant is indicative of Level 5.

5 a) Just over 1cm. The degree of accuracy expected in reading information from this type of graph would be considered Level 4.

b) and c) Plant B, because the graph line is above that of A and is a steeper line therefore showing that the plant grew more quickly. These combined answers would gain one mark, indicative of Level 4/5.

d) One mark for any of the following – one plant had more heat/light/nutrients/water than the other. All

44 KS2 ReviseWise Science

indicative of Level 4/5. An answer that showed awareness of genetic differences, e.g. they are different species, would be Level 6 (this level is not expected of primary school pupils).

Classifying materials (page 23)

1 i)–vi) Object chosen should show knowledge of a range of materials and why they are used for that particular purpose. For example, wooden handle on a spoon, because the wood does not conduct heat as well as metal; glass for a drinking container, so that the contents can be seen; steel for a fork, because it is strong and rigid.

Knowledge of materials and their use for particular objects indicates Level 3.

2 Ring around wooden pencil and plastic pen.

3 Ring around key, saucepan and ring.

4 Metal is strong, rigid and can be shaped into different objects. (All Level 3.)

Investigating magnetism and electricity (page 24)

1 a) False b) True c) False d) True e) False. All correct indicative of Level 4.

2 Steel knife, steel can and iron nail all ticked. Any wrong answers would mean the mark would not be allocated. Knowledge that not all metals are magnetic is Level 3, with an ability to name specific non-magnetic metals indicative of Level 4.

3 Ring around steel and iron. Although graphite conducts electricity it is not magnetic. Correct answer here indicative of Level 4.

Solids, liquids and gases (page 25)

1 a) water vapour b) melting c) helium d) water
e) condensation f) solid g) liquid h) metals
i) evaporation j) gases

Evaporating in everyday life (page 26)

1 Any sensible estimation, e.g. 2–6 hours, depending on the prevailing weather conditions. On a summer day at about 17°C a puddle of this size takes about 2 hours to disappear completely.

2 The water has evaporated, i.e. changed from a liquid to a gas. Knowledge that although a puddle disappears, water does not **disappear**, it changes state from a liquid to a gas. Using the word "disappear" in relation to water in this context would not get a mark.

3 The warmer the day the quicker the puddle will evaporate. Being able to make a generalisation like this is indicative of Level 5.

4 The one in the cool room. Straight read-off from the graph – indicative of Level 3.

5 The cool room. Answer should show an understanding of the different graph lines. The flannel left in a cool room for 4 hours would have the highest mass (i.e. still retain the most water). Indicative of Level 4.

6 10g. After 2 hours the flannel in the hot radiator did not lose any more mass due to the evaporation of water. Therefore the flannels must have weighed 10g to start with. Interpreting results like this is indicative of Level 4/5.

Making a solution (page 27)

1 a) Sugar dissolves in both cold and hot water, but it dissolves more quickly in hot water.

b) Salt dissolves in both cold and hot water, but it dissolves more quickly in cold water.

c) Chalk does not dissolve in either cold or hot water. Although it mixes with the water it can be seen to settle to the bottom after a few moments.

d) Wax does not dissolve in cold or hot water, but does **melt** in hot water.

e) Tea dissolves partially in cold and hot water – the water changes colour, showing that something has dissolved, but the leaves remain visible, showing that they have not dissolved.

f) Bicarbonate of soda dissolves in both cold and hot water, but it dissolves more quickly in hot water.

Making accurate observations and recording these is indicative of Level 3/4.

2 A small patch of sugar can be seen. Knowing that this is showing that dissolving sugar is a reversible change is indicative of Level 4.

3 The water has evaporated into the air. Use of specific terms like 'evaporation' and knowing what happens when liquid water turns into water vapour is indicative of Level 4/5.

Reversible and irreversible changes (page 28)

1 Melting 2 Dissolving 3 Melting
4 Dissolving 5 Dissolving 6 Melting
7 Melting 8 Melting

Getting all of the above correct, i.e. recognising melting and dissolving in a number of different contexts, is indicative of Level 5.

9–15 10 Candle wax melting, 12 margarine being heated to melt, 13 water changing to water vapour and 15 water changing to ice all ticked, shows an understanding of reversible changes in a range of contexts which is indicative of Level 5. Only some correct would be Level 4.

Separating a mixture (page 29)

1 Ring around **both** magnet and funnel and filter paper (or sieve). Filter paper is a better answer than sieve, but as long as there is an understanding that for the sieve to be of use the holes would have to be very small so as to trap the sand and iron filings, and not let them pass through with the water. Indicative of Level 3.

2 a) Filter/sieve the mixture to separate the solids that have not dissolved from the water and sugar solution.

b) Separate the 2 solids in the filter paper/sieve from each other by using a magnet to attract the iron filings, leaving the sand behind.

c) Separate the sugar from the water by allowing the water to evaporate, leaving the solid sugar behind. This process could be speeded up by heating/placing somewhere hot, like on top of a radiator.

A full explanation that is completely correct would be indicative of Level 5. Knowing some parts would be indicative of Level 3/4.

Electricity drawings and symbols (page 30)

1 ⊗ is the symbol for a bulb.

2 ▽ is the symbol for a buzzer.

3 ∣∣ is the symbol for cell. (Commonly called a battery – but in science terms, a battery is a number of cells joined together.)

4 This symbol is a motor. —(M)—

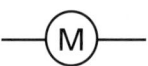

5 This symbol is a switch. ——/——

To know all these symbols correctly is indicative of Level 5.

6 David's circuit diagram:

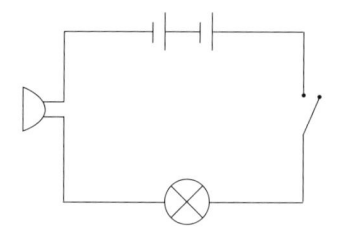

Correctly drawn symbolic circuit with the 2 cells, correctly aligned i.e. plus/minus, plus/minus and other components correct with no gaps would probably gain 2 marks, whereas showing only one cell with everything else correct would probably gain 1 mark – indicative of Level 5.

Looking at switches (page 31)

1 a) Pressing your finger on the plastic knob makes the metal underneath touch the metal strip on the bottom.

b) Moving the switch to the left makes the piece of metal underneath touch the raised piece of metal on the right.

2 When the 2 pieces of metal are touching inside a switch, the electricity can flow through the circuit, because metal conducts electricity. This will cause a bulb to light or a buzzer to sound – or whatever is connected in the circuit to work.

Friction (page 32)

1 The push from your hand makes the coin move.

2 Friction. Being able to name forces is indicative of Level 4.

3 The polished table top – because all the distances here are greater than the distances moved by the coin on the ordinary table top. Indicative of Level 3.

4 The bigger the force, the further the coin moves. This type of question requires an answer that identifies the two factors asked for and correctly makes a generalisation about their relationship. Two marks are usually awarded for this type of answer, which is indicative of Level 5. If a simpler explanation of one instance is given, e.g. when it is pushed hard it goes a

long way, one mark is usually awarded. If the factors are changed in the answer, e.g. the harder it is pushed the faster it goes, no marks are awarded.

Know your forces (page 33)

Across 1 balanced 4 force-meter 6 size 7 upthrust
8 down 9 newton

Down 2 air resistance 3 gravity 4 force
5 friction

Investigating forces (page 34)

1 The larger the surface in contact with the water, the harder it is to push the object under the water, so a large inflated balloon is probably the most difficult of the objects suggested. The upthrust of the water can easily be felt. Observation and description of this sort is indicative of Level 3. Using the term 'upthrust' indicates Level 4.

2 The object 'jumps' back up to the surface of the water. This is because the water pushes up against the object. (It floats because the upthrust and gravity are balanced.) This is indicative of Level 4, with understanding of forces in balance – Level 5.

3 Mass: 32 kg, Weight 320 N; 38 kg, 380 N; 21 kg, 210 N; 30 kg, 300 N; 25 kg, 250N

4 a) Force **b)** The length of spring. Being able to correctly identify both factors is indicative of Level 5.

Pushing and pulling (page 35)

2 The finger is pushing down on the spring and the spring is pushing up on the finger.

3 Gravity is pulling the paper down, and air resistance/friction is pushing up against the sheet of paper.

Getting 2 & 3 correct is indicative of Level 4; a partial answer, mentioning only of one of the forces and direction is more indicative of Level 3.

4 The hand is pushing onto the sponge and the sponge is pushing back against the hand.

Getting this one correct is indicative of Level 5 because the object involved is not moving and the understanding of the sponge pushing against the hand is more complex than forces in moving situations.

5 She should exert a force on the right hand side of the see-saw, either by pushing down on it with her hand or by placing a mass heavier than 100g on the opposite end of the see-saw so that the weight is greater than the left-hand side.

Investigating light (page 36)

1 Source of light – torch, candle, Sun, lamp-post, car headlamp, firework, computer screen.

All of these answers correct is indicative of Level 3 because there is a generalised understanding about light sources and objects that reflect light.

2 The mirror reflects light which enters Josh's eyes – ticked. Knowledge and understanding of this is indicative of Level 5.

3 Not as much of the room can be seen because the light from other objects is blocked by the tube and so less light is entering your eye. Correct answer show an understanding that we see objects when light from them enters our eyes, indicative of Level 5.

A closer look at light (page 37)

1 The shadow is much darker and larger than when it is far away from the surface. This is because more of the light is blocked by the object when it is close to the surface, preventing light from reaching that area of ground or wall. Correct answer indicative of Level 4.

2 a) Opaque **b)** Transparent **c)** Opaque
d) Translucent **e)** Transparent **f)** Opaque
g) Translucent **h)** Opaque.

Knowledge of all these materials and the correct terminology is indicative of Level 3/4.

3 A dark shadow shows that little or no light is reaching that area – it is being blocked by the object.

4 A faint shadow shows that some light is passing through the object (or sometimes where the light source is a very long way away from the opaque object, reflected light is reaching the area – this is beyond the requirement of Key Stage 2).

Correct answers to 3 and 4 indicate Level 4.

Making noise (page 38)

1 Because the cling film is vibrating. Knowledge that the sound waves travelling through the air can make another object vibrate is indicative of Level 4.

2 The air. Knowing that vibrations from sound sources

require a medium to travel through indicates Level 4.

3 Because the vibrations travel through the tray to your hand as well as through the air.

4 In this order only: E Piccolo, A Flute, C Clarinet, D Saxophone B Bassoon.
Recognising that the length of the instrument affects the pitch of the notes produced is indicative of Level 3/4. Explaining how to alter the pitch of a note would be Level 5.

Owl's question: Why can't you hear any noise in space? Answer: because there is no air in space so there's nothing for the sound waves to travel through.

Good vibrations (page 39)

1 No. From the table it can be seen that the pencils being hit together could be heard over a greater distance than the pin dropped on the book. To be able to provide a simple explanation of a pattern in results is indicative of Level 3.

2 The louder the sound, the further away you can hear it. Correctly describing the 2 factors is indicative of Level 5 and is usually awarded 2 marks. An answer that simply says "You can hear a loud sound a long way away" gets one mark, because it is giving one correct example of the 2 factors involved, but not making the generalisation. If the answer said "The more vibrations there are, the further away you hear it" there would be no marks because "more vibrations" does not necessarily refer to loudness (it could refer to pitch).

The Earth in space (page 40)

1 B ticked, indicative of Level 4

2 a) Sun b) Light from Sun c) Earth d) Day time
e) Night time.

All correct showing a simple understanding of day and night, Level 3/4. To be able to explain how movement of the Earth results in day and night is Level 5.

3 A useful mnemonic is My Very Easy Method Just Speeds Up Naming Planets. Knowledge of the order of planets in our solar system is indicative of Level 6 and is **not** required for Key Stage 2 tests.

Sun, Earth and Moon (page 41)

1 Ravi. Knowing that the Earth orbits the Sun is indicative of Level 3.

2 Because the Earth spins on its axis once every 24 hours and so the stationary Sun appears to be the one moving. Correct answer indicative of Level 4/5.

3 28 days. Level 3.

4 One complete turn/a rotation/one spin on its axis. The answer "a day" would not get a mark because the question asked about a **movement**. Level 4.

5 Matching: a) to v), b) to ii), c) to iv),
d) to i), e) to iii). All correct indicative of Level 4.